Published 1987
by Merehurst Press
5, Great James Street
London WC1N 3DA
by arrangement with
Temps de Pose Editions
12 rue de Sévigné
75004 PARIS
TELEX 215 313 F

© 1987 Editions Temps de Pose
© Copyright 1987 photographs : Pierre TOUTAIN
© Copyright 1987 text : Frédéric BARREYRE
ISBN 0-948075-65-1

Layout : Corinne REYMOND
Photocomposition : Graphelec Paris
Printed in Italy by SAGDOS-Brugherio-Milano
Translated by Veronica HAMMOND

QUEBEC

Photographs
Pierre TOUTAIN

Text
Frédéric BARREYRE

MEREHURST PRESS
LONDON

The art of living. Business acumen

First of all there was Hochelaga, an Indian village, discovered by Jacques Cartier. The French tur-ned it into Ville Marie, which became Mont-Royal, then Montreal. The ever-illuminated city is both the heart and the bank of Quebec.

Bringing wood to life

The "peasant artists" carve these serious faces to keep boredom at bay during the interminable winter months.

The descendants of the conquerors

450 years after Cartier, sails are hoisted again. In 1984 sailors from Quebec headed once more for St. Malo across the Atlantic.

The garden of Candide

"These few acres of snow are not worth the blood of a single French Grenadier," Voltaire wrote in his novel *Candide*, feeling that it was an absurd waste of money to contest English possession of Canada, a land twice the size of China. It must be noted that at that time the Iroquois were allied to the English and the Hurons to the French, and that both tribes excelled at European warfare, a fact which detracted from the image of the noble savage so popular during the century of the Enlightment. Sieur Arouet had not realized that the French Grenadiers were in fact defending Candide's garden. Candide is still cultivating his garden in the 1980s, while Pangloss has only the ever-fluctuating market price of otter and beaver-skin to philosophize about.

Quebec is a land in the wings of History whose citizens would appreciate advancing occasionally to the front of the stage. The situation is extremely difficult when one is so close to the domineering United States and to the Ontarian English, who are more English than the English, especially when they are Scots ! These are the people who direct the course of history, under the Union Jack and the Star-Spangled Banner, and who, from time to time, when necessary, allow the French Canadians, for glory alone, to take part in their gruesome games. For instance, to sacrifice their lives on the beaches of Dieppe, ostensibly to test the German defence system, in one of the most ill advised and futile operations of the Second World War. After that they were told to make their way home as quietly as possible to tap their maple trees. This is, of course, merely a rough outline of the situation. Nevertheless, since the time of Montcalm, Quebeckers have been living through a semi-covert existential crisis. Repeated but veiled hints, which are far more unpleasant that direct criticism, insinuate that all their history is in the past, that they have no present and no future. With sombre Hegelian ferociousness, they constantly attempt to transform that past, to galvanize it into a future. They are, to borrow the words of the German philosopher, "conscious of their unhappiness".

Patriotic fervour in Quebec has nothing to do with age.

What exactly is their history ? Successive conquests, the fruits of which were constantly nipped in the bud ; France's abandoning of the country, then her conceding over the years a few political or cultural scraps. Every prerequisite for collective depression has been fulfilled. When the renowned French Canadian singer Gilles Vignault tells us throughout the year in his songs that his country is "in the grip of winter", that is exactly what he is trying to express. All this, understandably, makes people very sensitive. Conversations in the countless bars of Montreal can be friendly, people can give a hearty welcome to the foreigner, even to the "damned Frenchie", but the latter must be extremely cautious, must choose his words with circumspection, must take the greatest care never to show a hint of cultural imperialism. He must never say, for example, that France has been waiting since "Maria Chapdelaine" for a great French-Canadian literary work, that the singer Charlebois is fine, but we're hoping for something to come. That the Canadian "idiom" dates back to the archaic language of Molière. An unpleasantly sharp reply will flash back that in the nineteenth century, if we take books as a example, only religious works were distributed in French Canada, the Bible plus a few devotional works ; that Flaubert and Hugo were unknown ; that France sent no literature to Canada; and that no-one can deny that France did not care a fig about Canada. And the speaker goes on to the history of his abandoned country.

Battered by wind and tides a God-fearing people nestle round the church.

*The countryside and
the faces of Quebec
reflect those of
rural France.*

A ribbon of asphalt through the fields

French Canadians call these strips of age-old nostalgia " Beauce" , after the region of France.

Thomas Raymond ploughs his land with horses, the ancestors of which came over with Jacques Cartier.

The sanctuary of European animals

The pioneers' bow

The left-handed fiddler brings to life the doleful songs and ballads of the conquerors of the New World.

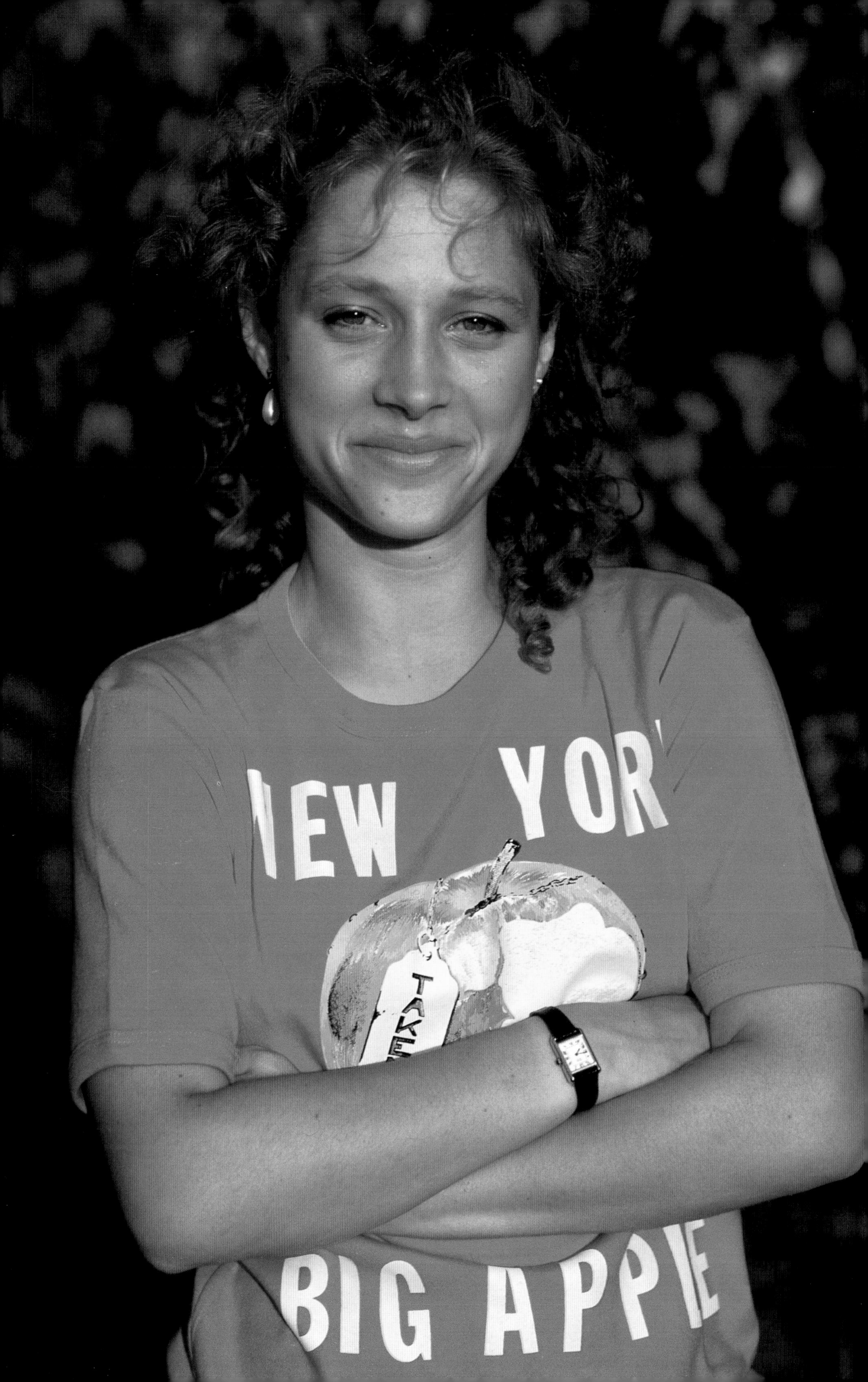
IEW YOR
TAKE
BIG APP

All Quebeckers are both
attracted and repelled by
their next-door neighbour America.
Every day the choice
has to be made between
the country of lakes and
the pulsating Yankee world.

An aquatic world

Quebec is the kingdom of water. The Montmorency Falls rival those at Niagara.

This thick forest provides over
a quarter of the world's
supply of paper.
A best-seller in the raw.

Amazonia in the Far North

The moose is the largest deer
in the world.
It is a model father
and husband who likes ...

*... to daydream with his family
under the scorched maple trees
of an Indian summer.*

*Their plumed headdresses
and their artistic and
cultural traditions
all scrupulously preserved,
the Indians represent the collective ...*

...guilty conscience of Canada.
The remorseful white man
has reduced them into
pathetic unaggressive idleness.

*Every totem demonstrates
the Indians' worship of
animals and of nature in general.*

*The creation of several
wild-life reserves
has prevented the American bison,
hunted down and destroyed
by the pioneers,
from becoming extinct.*

Liveliness in simplicity

*Modern artists in Quebec
have hotly refused to
follow European art.
Like Jean-Yves Coté,
they have experimented with
personal original styles.*

The Saint Lawrence River

A golden swathe under a stormy sky.

In the name of the King of France

In 1534 Jacques Cartier landed at Gaspé and laid claim to the territory in the name of Francis I of France. He had not come for that purpose, but had been seeking, in the steps of Columbus, a western route to the Indies. Today in Montreal people sometimes say he should have landed further south and discovered Louisiana. This is said in the depths of winter, when the temperature is minus thirty degrees celsius, the Saint Lawrence River is full of ice floes and the skidoo (invented in the 1920s by Bombardier, the engineer) and the plane are the only possible means of transport in the north of the country. So Cartier took over a small part of Quebec in the name of Francis I. Seventy-four years later Champlain, the lieutenant-general of New France, founded the town of Quebec. Several years passed before Paul Chomedy de Maisonneuve founded Ville Marie, which was to become Montreal. In 1690 its governor Frontenac repelled the English fleet which was besieging Quebec, a great success for New France. The mother-country, in spite of the distance, was determined to protect her Canadians. In 1697, following the treaty of Ryswick, New France received all the explored territory north of Mexico, another triumph for the province.

But kings die and new kings succeed. After 1697, Paris had other more pressing interests. At the beginning of the eighteenth century, to ensure peace in Europe, Versailles started to sell off Canada piecemeal. The treaty of Utrecht in 1713 was a momentous date. In the Dutch polders, the French yielded up Acadia, Hudson Bay and Newfoundland to the English. Although Montcalm fought like a lion and killed his victorious opponent, General Wolfe, just before he himself died, the town of Quebec fell to the English in 1759. After that there were only rearguard actions with short-lived successes. The far-flung dispersion of the Acadians of New Orleans... the 1783 Treaty of Versailles which made 6,000 French loyalists flee to Ontario... And during the nineteenth century the winning back by the French Canadians, alone and resolute, fragment by fragment and item by item, of institutions and land taken over by English. Thus, in 1867 French became the joint official language of the Ottawa Parliament, on a par with English. This was no insignificant gain, but rather a fantastic achievement. The Quebeckers persevered patiently and attained their end, by gnawing away at it. How incredibly like their beavers they are !

Montreal : an illuminated but precarious temple of prosperity.

40

Quebec was won back without help from Paris, Montreal remained French in spite of everything, without French intercession. These are the sources of Quebec's claim to have a separate identity. The French, who scoff at the antique "Jouanne" dialect of Montreal, do not generally understand this claim. The Americans, who visit Quebec as if it were a zoo with the tacit or avowed intention of taking it over, ignore it altogether. To make things worse, the Quebeckers lack the two crucial features of states seeking a degree of independence : poverty and military oppression. Most Quebeckers are well-off and enjoy the dual benefit of living under British law, with its respect for the individual, and of speaking the language of France where human rights were born. How curious it is ! Two sources of liberty flowing into frustration. Neither Hegel nor Marx could have foreseen such a situation. To understand it properly, let us visit Montreal and listen to Montreal.

Their name is Latraverse or Dugay. They say they are "pure wool". But many of them have a Huron grandmother, an Italian uncle and a Hungarian mother-in-law. They live in a city whose architecture is fundamentally Anglo-saxon. Metal steps up to semi-detached houses. Red-brick, cathedral-like administrative buildings, of the same type as one finds in Bombay. I forget who said, "In Montreal you are always in a minority group compared to someone else", meaning that Montreal is even more cosmopolitan a city than Toronto. Italian, Greek, Turkish and partly English too. The omnipresence of drinking places is symptomatic of a society in quest of its identity, of a city suffering from an existential uneasiness. Just like West Berlin, one could say, where existence is no easy matter. To pursue the comparison further, we could assert that Montreal is circled by two walls. A linguistic wall and that other wall of the surrounding desert. Oppression by sound, oppression by void.

Just beyond the city, which is unattractive but possesses the disquieting charm of a fortified camp resigned to its riches, lie over a thousand square miles. 300 miles from Montreal there is not a soul around. However, under the feet of the crazy madmen who have elected to live in the Great North, lie the world's largest gold reserve (practically unexplored), probably some oil, and various metal ores, most of them rare. A yet untapped source of wealth.

Here the pub is a dream. One desires to escape from these bricks into outer space.

42

The tides of fortune

The Saint Lawrence River carries into the heart of Montreal, the island town, the cargo ships which have ensured its prosperity for the past three centuries.

The extraordinary union
of typically British architecture
with a setting straight
out of central Europe.

A silken river

The life-giving waters of the Saint Lawrence River lap against Montreal.

Prisoners of winter

When the temperature is down to minus 35 degrees celsius the bars in the old town of Quebec are the sole havens in a wintry existence.

The austere crystalline architecture of the financial empire.

Underneath the winter snow, the beach

On a wall in Hull, an artist has painted the dream of all Quebeckers from October to April.

French City in an Anglo-Saxon World

*Junk shops furnish
the stuff of lonely
people's dreams.*

The trumpets of fame

A legendary police force

There are only seventy-seven Mounties left. One hundred years ago there were three hundred to uphold law and order in the vast open spaces of Canada.

*One man is proudly wearing
a fleur-de-lis.
Another one is playing
the bagpipes in a kilt.
Both speak French.*

The French die-hards
with their Louis XVth
tricorns uphold
a tradition and defy amicably
the saxophone of the British Empire.

The lights of history

French Canada has about six and a half million inhabitants, four million of whom live in Montreal. Another interesting figure is that 85% of the population of Quebec lives in the South, massed against the frontier with the United States. This gives rise to a collective attitude of withdrawal, of needing to please and to be liked by others which is utterly moving. At the same time, people intimate in the course of conversation that if everything went wrong, if they lost their job, if the threat of an atomic war hangs over the world or if, more matter-of-factly, the woman they love has gone off with a company director from Atlanta, the solution is quite simple — they would take their car and rush off to the North, alone, to seek refuge in solitude, to forget and to be forgotten among those astoundingly beautiful landscapes.

The fact is that Quebec is very beautiful, like all countries in which water is the predominant element. First of all, there is the Saint Lawrence, that river which is an inland sea. Then the lesser rivers and the lakes, which cover the equivalent of half the surface of France. An aquatic spirit prevails. Whoever lives on the water, whoever watches the water, whoever plunges his hand into water, sees eternity in a different way from those who can only feel fully at ease on the sand dunes of Téneré. The French Canadians have been up in arms frequently these last few years, but in my opinion, the expression of their legitimate grievances has been both steeled and moderated by all that water, still freezing cold in August, with its deep mysterious permanence. A revolution has never been launched on a lake.

One day in July 1967 Charles de Gaulle, who was, and this cannot be stressed too often, one of the greatest humorists of this century, climbed up the "mountain" of Montreal. He could see hardly anything but a colourful blur. In front of his dying eyes flashed the last stroboscopic lights of history. He could feel that he was being carried forward. But whither ? With his extraordinary sense of an historic situation, he shouted from the balcony of the Town Hall, "Long Live Free Quebec".

No-one understood this heartfelt call. It had, of course, nothing to do with any petty political slogan. He had not intented his few words to denote approval of any liberation movement. He was not exhorting Quebeckers to break with the Crown. He was extolling a certain feeling of personal freedom, he was restoring self-respect to hundreds of thousands of Frenchspeakers who had been disposed of, dirt cheap, by the locksmith of Versailles, Louis XVI. I learnt from an official source that he

Songs and poets for ambassadors.

68

The beautiful province

H. CAMPBELL &
THE DUROCHER
FARM COMMITTEE

Cure for boredom

Drinkers and smokers can assuage their craving 24 hours a day.

*The adventurous spririt of
Quebec has vanished
from the steep streets of
the old town of Quebec
to the shops of Hull.*

The American muddle

*The French of Molière
is but a flimsy bulwark
against the American invasion.*

*A people overwhelmed by
the immensity of its territory ...*

... contemplates its own image constantly,
as it is doing here at Mont Royal.

Good old jazz, with no holds barred

*Forests painted on concrete
to offset the solitude
of the city.*

*On the walls the padded
violence of ice-hockey.*

The heart of New France

Quebec, the oldest fortified city of North America, stands on the bank of the Saint Lawrence River. It is here that the saga of the New World French began.

A passion : the sun

On the lawns of Mont-Royal, with the return of spring, young people frolic on the green carpet of grass.

There are several ways
of saluting the return of spring.

The Gaspé peninsula,
that region called
"Peace of heart".

The white plains of Abraham

It is here in the centre of Quebec city that Montcalm was mortally injured at the head of his army. That day the English destroyed the dream of a French Canada.

The language of the rights of man

found his own words vastly amusing and that he, an old man with the heart of a child, was fond of stealing an occasional pot of jam that his opponent had hidden on the top shelf of the cupboard. In any case, it was a mere flash in the pan. Gilles Vignault and a few remarkable films came to France, and that was all. The true free Quebec is rooted in the soil, it is very pragmatic. It is epitomized by the "Caisses Populaires Desjardins", a unique type of savings bank. It is also a certain conception of human rights, the acceptance of a multi-racial population (yes, I know, they do have plenty of room, but all the same). It is Silicon Valley technology, little-known worldwide. French Canada is a raccoon perpetually fluffing up its sleek, well-nourished pelt.

However, it is true that when a Quebecker has amassed enough money, he goes down to the southernmost point of the United States, where it is warm. National feeling is like a tenuous optical fibre which occasionally fails to link up all the canals of the eye. Yet the scenery is breathtaking. Jacques Cartier kept a diary, a pessimistic story. He wrote the following : "If the soil were as excellent as the harbours, it would be ideal. This place should not be called Newfoundland, but new-found terrifying jagged rocks and stones... I consider that this is the land which God gave to Cain." How false his impression was !

However, we can make allowances for Cartier, tossed about in his little birchwood boat. What does Quebec actually represent today, if we leave its doubts and perplexities behind us ? Twenty per cent of the world's pulp for paper ; iron ore, lithium, titanium, and especially gold. The general attitude is : keep all outsiders away from our natural resources. We want neither the Americans nor the English Canadians. It is not a very romantic attitude, but, if you discuss the point with any Quebecker, a reaction of self-protection which has replaced the desire for independence. A desire to hold on to one's own, which Quebeckers try to reconcile with the need to be liked, the need to create, the need for their works to be circulated. An insoluble problem which America and France cannot understand. The combination of existential perplexities with an economic boom is literally unbearable. And yet these French Canadians' lives go on and they live well.

They dance, drink and live out, from day to day, that curious amalgam of American culture and the French way of life. They play base-ball and ice-hockey, the most violent sport ever invented with the exception of boxing. They fish in clear waters. People from different districts may not understand one another, since the English-speaker knows no French and the French-speaker has always refused to learn English, though he speaks it perfectly well, but does not wish to advertise the fact.

Quebec has marvellous restaurants, wonderful shows, and cosier cafés than those of Paris. The Quebeckers have won on their home-ground a battle lost by all other Northerners : in the teeth of the English and in spite of the snow, they have routed boredom.

The opaque transparency of life among the glaciers. Understanding a people hemmed in by winter and the ocean.

Labourers on the ice-fields

The ice-breaker ploughs on its way with hellish din.

The snowmobile, invented by J. Armand Bombardier, appeared in 1959: a new sport was born as well as one of the biggest Canadian firms, Bombardier Inc.

... then came the Ski-Doo

*Two objects for eternity,
the snow and the Indians.*

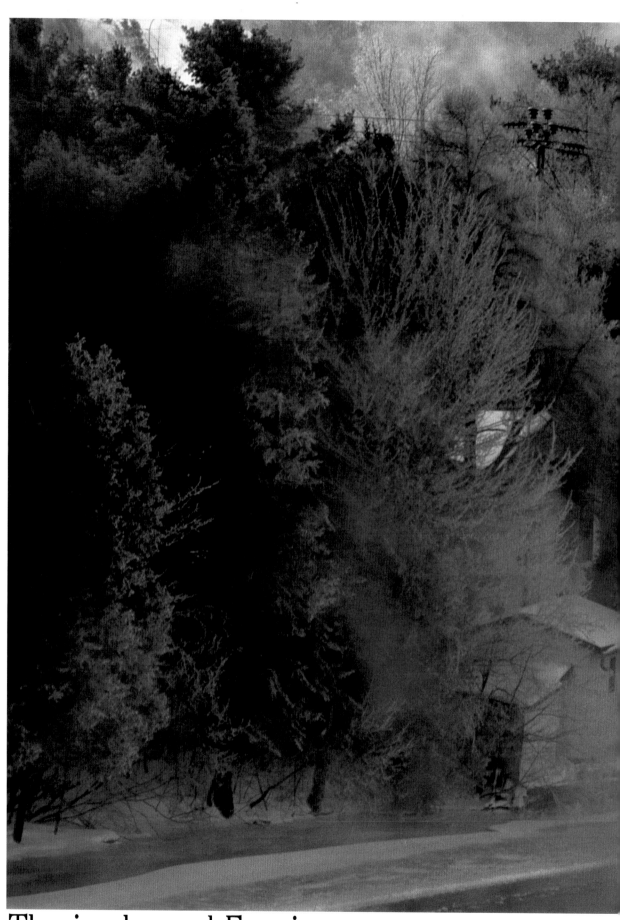

The ice-bound Empire

For six months of the year a shroud of ice covers forests, lakes and rivers.

The power of frost

General Motors climbs up the winter scene.

In Quebec nature still reigns

On either bank of these milky falls the land and the forest are still unexplored.

*A white desert in
the far north of the country.
Now mapped out ...*

*...it attracts trappers
in search of fox skins
of various colours.*

The descendants of warriors at rest

*Dreaming on the bank
of the Saint Lawrence,
the river of memories.*

In the Gaspé peninsula,
toiling sailors ...

*... and the homeliness
of primitive painting.*

113

A hollow eye on the green sea. Quebeckers still glance at the continent from which they came. A glance at the forgotten past with a smile for Jacques Cartier.

"It is a place not to be forgotten
or mixed up with other places..."
(Charles Dickens.)

In 1984, sea-cadets
from all over the world ...

... assembled to commemorate
Jacques Cartier's crossing.

The cathedrals of the sea

"Dar Mlodziezy"...under sail... hails the Gaspé coast.

121

A sure haven

"As we were sailing in good weather... it suited us to enter a harbour, which we named St. Catherine's." (Jacques Cartier)

"We took to our small boats to go to a cape of the land of the south which was the longest and the most pro-minent that we had ever seen at sea (the Saint Lawrence)." (Jacques Cartier)

"Je me souviens" (I remember),
the motto of Quebec.

ACKNOWLEDGEMENTS

Pierre Toutain
and Temps de Pose Editions
would particularly like
to thank the following:

In Quebec:
Nicole PAIEMENT
Line BLONDEAU, Hilton International Québec
Diane LORTIE
Jacques DENAULT
Richard LESSARD, Canadian coast-guard
Martine and Jean BAYEUR
Jocelyn and Jean-Yves COTE
Henry JAMET
Normand PRIEUR, Bombardier Inc.

In Paris:
Annie LOISELY, Tourisme Québec

TOURISME
QUÉBEC

Martine BENCHETRIT, Air Canada

A BREATH OF FRESH AIR   AIR CANADA

Nicole DONNAT
Corinne REYMOND
Colette CARRIERE
Pierre VALIQUETTE
Philippe GANIER RAYMOND
Fernando REHOYO
Guy Ducharme
The Macdonald Stewart Foundation

For their contribution
to the publication of this book